SANTORINI, GREECE

Travel Guide Book

A Comprehensive 5-Day Travel Guide to Santorini,
Greece & Unforgettable Greek Travel

• Travel Guides to Europe Series •

Passport to European Travel Guides

D0754013

❧

Eye on Life Publications

Santorini, Greece Travel Guide Book
Copyright © 2015 Passport to European Travel Guides

ISBN 10: 1519421621
ISBN 13: 978-1519421623

~

Other Travel Guide Books by Passport to European Travel Guides

Greece & the Greek Islands

Top 10 Travel Guide to Italy

Naples & the Amalfi Coast, Italy

Rome, Italy

Venice, Italy

Florence, Italy

Paris, France

Provence & the French Riviera, France

Top 10 Travel Guide to France

London, England

Barcelona, Spain

Amsterdam, Netherlands

Prague, Czech Republic

Berlin, Germany

Munich, Germany

Vienna, Austria

Istanbul, Turkey

Budapest, Hungary

Brussels, Belgium

"Greece is the most magical place on Earth."
—Kylie Bax

Table of Contents

• Map of Santorini, Greece •

© Photo Credit: Emmanouela Studios Santorini

• Introduction •

Santorini, Greece. **Thera.** A true cosmopolitan gem in the **sapphire waters** of the Aegean Sea! Come here, and you'll never want to leave. The **black sand beaches** and **luminous white buildings** with **powder-blue dome caps** make for a **spellbinding and picturesque** temptation to return again and again. Not bad for being all that remains of one of the most extreme volcanic eruptions in history, right?

In this 5-day guide to Santorini, you'll find a variety of our **top recommendations** and helpful tips to prepare you for having the best travel experience during your time in Greece! **Read over the insider tips** carefully and familiarize yourself with the information about preparing for your trip. **Every traveler** has different preferences, and we've included a wide range of recommendations to suit all tastes and budgets.

You're welcome to follow our detailed **5-day itinerary** to the letter, or you can **mix and match** the activities at your own discretion.

Most importantly, we know you're sure to enjoy the **beautiful island paradise** that is Santorini, Greece — and you'll certainly fall in love at first sight with all it waits to offer!

Do enjoy!

The Passport to European Travel Guides Team

.

• City Snapshot •

Language: Greek

Local Airports:

Athens International Airport
("Eleftherios Venizelos") or *Santorini (Thira) National Airport* (JTR), located north of the village of Kamari. Another option is *Heraklion International Airport* on the island of Crete.

Currency: Euro | € (EUR)

Country Code: 30

Emergencies: 112 (all emergencies within the European Union), 171 (tourist police), 100 (police), 199 (fire department), 166 (first aid, EMS). The emergency calls at 112 are answered in Greek, English, French, and German.

• Before You Go... •

✓ Have a Passport

If you don't already have one, you'll need to **apply for a passport** in your home country a good two months before you intend to travel, to avoid cutting it too close. **You'll need to find a local passport agency**, complete an application, take fresh photos of yourself, have at least one form of ID and pay an application fee. **If you're in a hurry**, you can usually expedite the application for a 2-3 week turnaround at an additional cost.

✓ Need a Visa?

You can use the following website to find out if you need a visa to enter **Greece**:
http://livingingreece.gr/2007/06/10/non-eu-countries-visa-free-travel-to-greece.

If you are a **US or Canadian citizen**, you are not required to apply for a visa unless you plan to stay in

Greece for **more than 90 days**. European citizens can enter Greece with only a national identity card.

The US State Department provides a wealth of country-specific information for American travelers, including **travel alerts and warnings**, the location of the **US embassy in each country**, and of course, **whether or not you need a visa** to travel there!
http://travel.state.gov/content/passports/english/country.html

✓ Healthcare

Most people neglect this, but it's important to keep in mind when traveling to any foreign country. It's wise to **consult with your doctor** about your travel plans and ensure **routine immunizations are current**. You want to protect against things like influenza, polio, chickenpox, mumps, measles, etc.

If you are a European citizen, a **European Health Insurance Card** (EHIC) covers you for most medical needs, **but not for non-emergencies**. The card is available from health centers and post offices throughout the European Union.

Citizens from other countries should find out if there is **a reciprocal arrangement for free medical care** between their home country and Greece. If you do have **insurance at home**, be sure to check with them about **traveler's coverage**. It's important to know how you'll pay for services in case of an emergency while you're away.

Give your insurance information and passport at the time services are rendered, and **save receipts and bills** so your insurance company can reimburse you if appropriate.

✓ Set the Date

Santorini is one of the only locations in Europe with a **desert climate**. There are basically two seasons in Santorini: **April to October** is the **warm, dry season**, and **November to March** is the **cold, rainy season**.

We think the best time to visit Santorini is in the fall, when the weather is generally warm **during the day** and there are fewer crowds. **Springtime** is beautiful but tends to be chilly, with windy temperatures that can dip into the 50s.

Most people visit Santorini during **the summertime**, so you need to book your hotel **at least two months** in advance if you plan on visiting between **June and August**.

Also note that most hotel **prices double** during the high season. So if you're looking for the best bargains, **wintertime** is your best bet, but expect a lot of rain and chill.

✓ Pack

• We recommend packing **only the essentials** for the season in which you're traveling. By far, the most important thing to pack is a good pair of **walking shoes** (walking boots or light, comfortable sandals and sneakers). Most streets in Santorini are made of cobblestone, so good walking shoes are necessary!

• Always **bring an umbrella** whenever you travel. **Unexpected showers** can often ruin a great day of sightseeing.

• **In the colder months**, bring a warm sweater, clothes that you can layer, and a rain jacket. And definitely don't forget **sunscreen, sunglasses, and a hat**.

• **A backpack** can be handy during the day when you go out sightseeing and collecting souvenirs, particularly when getting on and off buses, boats, trams, etc.

• **Travelers from outside Europe** will need to bring along a **universal electrical plug converter** that can work for both lower and higher voltages. This way you'll be able to plug in your cell phones, tablets, curling irons, etc., during the trip.

• **Although English** is spoken around tourist areas, **you'll likely encounter more people who only speak Greek**. So bring a **Greek phrase book** along with you so you can greet appropriately and ask common questions.

• **Hand sanitizer** is always great to have along with you when traveling.

• A simple **first aid kit** is always a good idea to have in your luggage, just in case.

• **Take pictures of your travel documents and your passport** and email them to yourself before your trip.

This can help in the unfortunate event they get lost or stolen.

• **Medication.** Don't forget to have enough for the duration of your trip. It's also helpful to have a **note from your physician** in case you're questioned for carrying a certain quantity.

• **Pack lightly**. Getting on and off planes, water taxis and ferries will be very tiring if you have lots of luggage.

✓ Phone Home

How will you call home from Santorini? Does your cell phone company offer service while abroad? **What are their rates?**

There are many ways to **call home** from Greece that are inexpensive or completely free.

You may also **sign up for roaming or Internet hotspots** through your own cell phone provider. You can also use Skype, WhatsApp, Viper, or many other voice-over IP providers that are entirely free.

Other options are to buy a Greek **phone chip** for your phone (which also gives you an Greek phone number), purchase **calling codes** before you leave home, or you can buy **calling cards** or **prepaid cell phones** once you arrive in Greece.

✓ Currency Exchange

Greece uses the **euro** as its currency (same for most of Western and Central Europe). Check out the **currency exchange** rates prior to your trip. You can do so using the following or many other online currency exchange calculators, or through your bank. For the best rates, we recommend **waiting until you arrive in Greece** to buy euros.
http://www.xe.com/currencyconverter

Also, make sure your bank knows you'll be traveling abroad. This way you avoid having foreign country transactions flagged and declined, which can be extremely inconvenient.

✓ Contact Your Embassy

In the unfortunate event you should lose your passport or be victimized while away, **your country's embassy** will be able to help you. Be sure to give your itinerary and contact information to a close **friend or family member**, then contact your embassy with your emergency contact information before you leave.

✓ Your Mail

Ask a neighbor to **check your mailbox** while you're away or visit your local post office and request a hold. **Overflowing mailboxes** are a dead giveaway that no one's home.

• Getting in the Mood •

Here are a few great books and movies **set in Santorini** that we recommend you watch in preparation for your trip to this magical and dreamy locale!

• What to Read

One really good novel to read about Santorini is _The Santorini Odyssey_ by Peg Maddocks. It's a story about four Americans who voluntarily participate in the exploration of a cave damaged by an earthquake and discovered by locals in the ruins of Thera.

Another good read for familiarizing yourself with Santorini's origins is Walter Friedrich's _Fire in the Sea: The Santorini Volcano: Natural History and the Legend of Atlantis._ Santorini was home to one of the most intensely studied volcanoes in history; and it supported the thriving Minoan civilization up until a huge eruption about 3,600 years ago. It's a fascinating read that we think puts you in the mood to discover the locations described in person.

• What to Watch

Summer Lovers is a 1982 film starring **Peter Gallagher and Daryl Hannah**, shot on location in Santorini. Michael (Gallagher) and his childhood sweetheart Cathy (Hannah) travel to Greece to spend the summer in Santorini, where Michael finds himself enchanted by another woman, despite his love for Cathy. He becomes torn between the two, and you won't believe where things go from there — **it's definitely worth a watch!**

• Local Tourist Information •

As soon as you arrive at the airport, train station or ferry port in Santorini, you can pick up brochures, city maps, and other helpful information from the regional tourism board. You can also **ask any questions you might have** and rest assured that a friendly, English-speaking attendant will be happy to help.

The local **tourist bureaus** can provide you with information about everything from Santorini's public and private transportation, to upcoming special events happening in the city.

Also, most hotels in Santorini have maps available for guests as well as a variety of tips about area restaurants, museums, and seasonal events.

• About the Airports

If you arrive at the **Athens International Airport** (Eleftherios Venizelos), there are a few options for continuing on to Santorini. Either take a nice leisurely 8-hour ferry ride, or a 5-hour "Flying Dolphin" ride (both from the port in Piraeus or Rafina), or you can take a 45-50 minute flight to Santorini with the local airlines. **Athen's airport website is:** https://www.aia.gr/en/traveler

Santorini (Thira) National Airport is an airport in Santorini/Thira (JTR), just north of the village of Kamari. It serves as a military and civilian airport.
http://www.hcaa.gr/en/our-airports/kratikos-aerolimenas-santorinhs-kasr

Crete also has a small airport (**Heraklion International Airport**) that you can flight into en route to other Greek islands.
http://www.hcaa.gr/en/our-airports/kratikos-aerolimenas-hrakleioy-n-kazantzakhs

• How Long is the Flight?

<u>To Athens:</u>

• **The flight to Athens from New York City** is approx. 10 hours

• **From London** is approx. 3.5 hours

• **From Hong Kong** is approx. 15 hours

• **From Moscow** is approx. 4 hours

• **From Sydney** is approx. 21.5 hours

• **From Toronto** is approx. 10 hours

• **From Beijing** is approx. 14 hours

• **From Paris** is approx. 3.5 hours

• **From Cape Town** is approx. 16.5 hours

<u>To Santorini:</u>

• **From New York City** is approx. 11.5 hours

- **From London** is approx. 6 hours
- **From Hong Kong** is approx. 16.5 hours
- **From Moscow** is approx. 6 hours
- **From Sydney** is approx. 24 hours
- **From Toronto** is approx. 12.5 hours
- **From Beijing** is approx. 14.5 hours
- **From Paris** is approx. 3.5 hours
- **From Cape Town** is approx. 18.5 hours

• Overview of Santorini •

The island of **Santorini** (Greek: Σαντορίνη, Thera) is located in the southern Aegean Sea, part of the Cyclades island group and covers about twenty-eight square miles. What you see as Santorini today is essentially what remains of an enormous volcanic eruption that destroyed the island's earliest settlements, and created the current geological caldera, a cauldron-like formation left after the collapse of the land from a volcanic eruption.

Only two of Santorini's six islands are inhabited, and tourists typically spend most of their time on the largest island, **Thira**. Sitting just off the main island's northwest coast is the smaller and less populated (as well as less touristy) island of **Thirassia**.

In addition to the **delicious cuisine, pretty wineries and strong reds**, there are also **plenty of historical sites** to learn about and explore in Santorini.

One thing's for sure — a vacation in Santorini is **guaranteed to cast a spell on you** with its **stunning sunsets and sunrises, beautiful whitewashed houses with powder blue domes**, and the most mesmerizing, **sapphire seawaters** in the world.

You can choose to relax on the **black sand beaches** or spend hours out sightseeing — either way, we know you're in for the trip of a lifetime!

• Insider Tips For Tourists •

Etiquette

• **Walking Etiquette:** There are very few sidewalks in most towns in Santorini, so **be careful while walking about these narrow**, steep streets and passageways. You may need to give way to the occasional speeding scooter, or step aside for a donkey.

• **Dining Etiquette:** Be sure to eat everything on your plate, especially if invited to someone's home. If you know you won't be able eat everything on your plate, tell the hostess it's too much right away.

• **Body Language Etiquette:** Avoid causing unintentional offense in Greece with these gestures: 1) Holding your palm out to someone, and 2) Making the "OK" sign: forming a circle with your thumb and forefinger — both gestures are considered to be very rude in the culture.

• **Nodding your head** "yes" or shaking your head "no" may not always be understood in Greece. Locals generally just move their head forward slightly for "yes," and move it slightly backward for "no."

• **Touring Etiquette:** One of Greece's biggest plagues is the abundance of stray dogs — they're everywhere. So beware the dogs and avoid petting or feeding them.

• **Drinking Etiquette:** Greeks like to drink alcohol but they expect decent behavior even while under influence. The legal drinking age in Greece is eighteen; and sixteen with adult supervision.

As for drinking water in Greece: the water is drinkable in most areas of the mainland, but on the islands, it's best to drink bottled water only. Most of the islands lack a sufficient water supply, so water is imported for every day living — bathing, doing laundry, etc.

Time Zone

Santorini is in the Eastern European Time Zone (GMT+3). There is a **7-hour time difference** between New York City and Santorini (Santorini is ahead). When it is 8:00 am in New York City, it is 3:00 pm in Santorini).

The format for abbreviating dates in Europe is different from the US. They use: **day/month/year**. So for example, August 23, 2035 is written in Europe as 23 August 2035, or 23/8/35.

Saving Time & Money

• **You can spend less on lunch** by buying yummy street food all over the island. **Gyros and souvlakis** are tasty, filling, and inexpensive. You can also snack on **refreshing coconuts** still in their shells, **fresh pastries**, and more!

• **Always double check your bill** in restaurants and ensure the prices reflect the ones on the menu.

• If you're planning to **island-hop**, the cost of taking inter-island ferries and/or water taxis can add up pretty quickly. So we recommend taking the **overnight ferries** — you can save up to 50% off the daytime rates, plus save the cost of the night's stay in a hotel.

• **Planning ahead** is always best when on a budget. If you book the ferries **at least two months in advance**, you can save up to 25% off the cost of your tickets.

• If you're on a tight budget, you might want to **avoid staying or dining in the town of Oia** because it's Santorini's most expensive area. But we do still encourage you to visit Oia, as it's certainly a beautiful town full of wonderful sights and attractions.

• If you visit Santorini in the **warmer months**, you can save money by **camping out** instead of booking a hotel or hostel. There are **two designated campsites** in Santorini, but you may notice that camping in places not designated for it is largely accepted in Greece. http://www.travel-to-santorini.com/camping

• **Rent a moped** for quick and easy transportation around the island that's less expensive and more convenient than renting a car or taking taxis from place to place. It's also a great way to explore the island's towns and cities more intimately. You can usually rent a moped for under $20 USD per day.

Tipping

Tipping is not mandatory in Greece, although most **taxi drivers** and **some wait staff** will expect it from tourists. **Restaurant bills** will already include a service charge, but if your service is remarkable and you're inspired to leave an additional tip, ask your server if they get to keep their tips before **rounding your bill** up a bit as a thank you, particularly when **paying in cash**; i.e., if your bill is €18.35, you can give €20. (Some restaurants do not allow their servers to keep tips, so whatever you left would just amount to paying more for the food.)

If you stay in a hotel for more than a couple of nights, it's appropriate to leave a few euros for the **chambermaid**.

When You Have to Go

"Where is the bathroom?" in Greek is: Parakalo, pou ine i tualetta? (Πού είναι η τουαλέτα)

Public toilets in Greece are pretty rare. The ones you do find may not be very clean. The better cafés, bars, restaurants and museums will usually have clean restrooms. You may have to buy a soft drink or small treat to use it in most restaurants and cafés.

Be aware that you generally cannot flush toilet paper down the toilet in Santorini. The sewage system cannot handle it. When you wipe, always remember to **throw the toilet paper in the waste bin or bag provided**. (There may be a few exceptions on the island, but not many.)

Taxes

In Europe, a **Value Added Tax (VAT)** is added to the majority of goods and services and should be incorporated in the advertised price. As of this writing, **VAT in Greece is 23%** for everything except certain items, such as food, books, newspapers and pharmaceuticals, which can range from 6.5%-16%.

If you live outside of Europe, you can be reimbursed for private, non-commercial purchases that included VAT and exceed about $80 USD. **For tourists**, VAT is refunded on purchases taken out of the country.

When you shop in locations bearing a "Tax Free Shopping" or "Tax Refund" logo, ask for a **stamped refund form + your receipt**. You will have up to **five months from the date of purchase** to present the form with your receipts to the custom's office at the airport. The refund can be paid out in cash, as a credit on your credit card, or you can have a check mailed to your home address.

Important to note that items like food, gasoline, alcohol and cigarettes **are not eligible** for a tax refund.

Phone Calls

The **country code** for Greece is 30.

When calling home from Santorini, first dial 00. You will then hear a tone. Then dial the country code (1 for the U.S. and Canada, 44 for the UK, 61 for Australia, 7 for Russia, 81 for Japan, and 86 for China), then the area code **without the initial 0**, then the actual phone number.

It can be expensive to call internationally **from a hotel** phone as they assess **heavy surcharges**. Therefore, buying a calling card may be your best bet for staying in touch in a cost-efficient way. There's also Skype, Google Talk, and free texting services like WhatsApp to **stay in touch without cost**.

Electricity

The electrical current in Greece is **220 volts** (for comparison, the US uses 120 volts), with standard European **two-prong plugs**. As previously mentioned, when traveling from outside Europe, you will need to bring an **adapter and converter** that will enable you to plug your electronics and appliances into the wall sockets. Cell phones, tablets and laptop chargers are typically **dual voltage** so you may not need a converter, just an adapter.

In Emergencies

You should keep the following phone numbers handy: 112 (any type of emergency), 171 (tourist police), 100 (police), 199 (fire department), 166 (ambulance). The emergency calls at 112 are answered in English, Greek, French, and German. We recommend noting these numbers, writing them down or emailing them to yourself if you have a smart phone.

Greek Phrases For Emergencies:

I am lost	Eho hathi
I need a doctor	Hirazome yiatro
Help!	Voithia!
Call the police!	Fonakste tin astinomia!
Call an ambulance!	Kaleste asthenoforo!
Where is the hospital?	Pou ine to nosokomio?

The Central Clinic of Santorini is a small medical clinic located near the bus station in Firá. It's open 24/7, but severe medical problems are evacuated to Athens: http://www.santair-cca.gr/en/santorini-central-clinic/

Pharmacies in Greece are open during **regular business hours** and closed on the weekends. A green cross outside marks the buildings. Each neighborhood has a 24-hour pharmacy.

Holidays

Every Sunday is a public holiday according to Greek law. **Other national holidays** are as follows:

• January 1 (New Year's Day)
• January 6 (Epiphany)
• February (Clean Monday/Shrove Monday/1st Day of Lent)
• March 25 (Annunciation/Independence Day)
• April (Good Friday/Easter)
• April (Easter Monday)
• May 1 (Labour Day)
• August 15 (Assumption/Dormition of the Holy Virgin)
• October 28 (Ochi Day)
• December 25 (Christmas Day)

• December 26 (Glorifying Mother of God)

Hours of Operation

Most of the banks in Santorini are found in the main square in Firá. Hours are typically limited to Monday through Thursday 8:00 am - 2:30 pm and 8:00 am - 2:00 pm on Fridays. In some areas, you may find a branch open longer in the evenings and on Saturday mornings.

Museums are generally closed on Mondays and stay open later in the summer months.

Store hours. Keep in mind that **Greek shop owners** siesta (rest) at noon, which can be inconvenient for tourists it is a well cherished local tradition.

Don't be surprised if everything's closed. **Many shops and small business** close for about **a week in August**, as well as many island hotels from **November until the middle of spring**.

Money

Greece uses the **euro** (€) as its currency (same for most of Western and Central Europe). The best way to get euros is to wait until you arrive in Greece and use your bankcard at any Greek ATM.

Most Greeks, especially in smaller towns, prefer to do business in **cash only**, so be sure to have some on hand at all times. However, we don't recommend having more than about **€200 in cash** at a time. This will minimize the damages in the unfortunate event your money is lost or stolen.

Most establishments accept credit cards but be mindful of **unnecessary fees,** such as being given the option of having your card charged in dollars vs. euros: **always choose euros**. Paying in dollars will usually cost you more in fees.

Climate and Best Times to Travel

As we mentioned, **Santorini has a hot climate**. There are basically two seasons: **April to October** is the **warm, dry season**, and **November to March** is the **chilly, rainy season**.

We think the best time to visit Santorini is in the fall, when the weather is warmer **during the day** and there are fewer crowds. **Springtime** is beautiful but tends to be chilly, with windy temperatures that can dip into the 50s.

Most people visit Santorini during the summertime, **June thru August**.

Winter months see lots of rain and chill, not ideal for sunning yourself on the beaches, but good for exploring the island and hiking. And don't forget your umbrella!

Transportation

Santorini has **two ports**: Athinios (Ferry Port) and Skala (Old Port). You can get to the capital city of Firá on foot, by cable car or scooter, and even by donkey.

There are usually lots of **taxis** waiting as the ferries dock, but if you come in late at night, we recommend arranging for **a taxi to pick you up** in advance. A taxi ride from the port to Firá takes about 15 minutes and is under €20.

The best means of **getting around in Santorini** is by **walking or taking the bus.** Walking is easy and convenient, but a bus is the best way to get from town to town. There are **KTEL bus routes** from Firá to various destinations around the main island. In the high season, buses run hourly from the airport to Firá.

If you plan to tour the **nearby islands**, you can catch a ferry from Athinios (about 5 miles south of Firá) or Ammoudi, which is near Oia. You can even hire a **water taxis**.

And again, you can also **hire a scooter, quad bike, or even a donkey** to get around!

Driving

There is no need (or much space) for driving around Santorini. You will get around mostly on foot, by bus, ferry, scooter or donkey, so renting a car is unnecessary; very few locals actually drive. Parking also becomes an issue in many areas, so **we don't recommend renting a car.**

However, in the event you should decide to **rent a car anyway**, please ensure you know all **motor vehicle regulations** and laws for driving in Greece. European driver's licenses are accepted for car rentals, but if you're not from Europe, be sure to get an **international driver's permit** before arriving in Greece: http://www.dmv.org/international-driver-permits.php

• Tours •

We've got some great recommendations for touring Santorini! Be sure to **check websites or call** for current rates and bookings.

By Bike

Santorini Adventures offers a great mountain bike tour called **Seaside Tour.** We think this is a great way to explore the island by bike! The tour is about four hours long and is tailored to your physical conditioning and preferences.

Santorini Adventures
Address: Epar.Od. Firon-Ormou Perissis, Santorini
Tel: +30 2286 036175
http://www.santoriniadventures.gr/seaside-tour.html

By Boat

For an intimate (and more expensive) experience of Santorini attractions, you can book a tour on a semi-private boat (yachts or catamarans accommodating 6 to 12 guests) with **Captain George** of **Santorini Yachting S/Y Eleftheria**! You can even charter the entire boat at an additional cost. We assure you that it's a scrumptiously gorgeous experience!

Santorini Yachting S/Y Eleftheria!
Address: Vlychada Marina, Vlychada, 84700, Greece
Tel: +30 694 441 0017
http://www.sy-eleftheria.com

Dakoutros Bros J.V. (Santorini Excursions) offers a great boat tour of the volcano! It's inexpensive and runs about three hours long. It's best to book this tour in advance. And for a more romantic experience, they also offer a sunset excursion you don't want to miss.

Santorini Excursions (Dakoutros Bros J.V.)
Address: Firá Central Square - 84700, Santorini
Tel: +30 22860 22958
http://www.santorini-excursions.com

By Bus

If riding around on a bus is more your style, there are several bus tours of Santorini available. Our top recommendation is **My Santorini's** _See Santorini in One Day_ bus and boat tour. The tour leaves at around 9:00 am and returns about thirty minutes after sunset. It's awesome!

Bus tours can be an enjoyable experience, but probably not as fun as seeing the island by boat or walking, that's why we like this one best!

My Santorini (Pelican Travel Services)
Address: Firá, Santorini, Firá, 84700, Greece
Tel: +30 22860 22220
http://www.mysantorini.com/See-Santorini-in-one-day-bus-and-boat-tour.html

Try Special Interest or Walking Tours

Are you a wine lover? <u>Santorini Wine Adventure Tours</u> is one of our favorite special interest tour experiences. You get to taste fine wines from some of the oldest vineyards in Europe! You can also learn to cook mouthwatering Greek dishes in a **six-hour cooking class** with the same company.

Booking a half-day **hiking tour** from Firá to Oia with **<u>Tours By Locals</u>** is the best option for hiking. You get to select your own guide, set your own pace and tell them exactly what you'd like to see around the island. This way you won't risk getting lost in the narrow and complicated little pathways in Santorini. Just **bring your camera** and be prepared to see dazzling sights!

How about seeing **Santorini by helicopter? Aegean Trails** offers private **<u>Santorini Day Tours</u>** by helicopter—have a breathtaking experience from the Greek skies!

<u>Pelican Travel Services</u> also offers a great **fishing tour** in Santorini's caldera!

And if diving is your thing, they also offer an amazing **diving tour** around the caldera!

Location Information:

Santorini Wine Adventure Tours
Address: Firá, 84700, Greece
Tel: +30 6932 960062 or +30 22860 34123
http://www.winetoursantorini.com

Tours By Locals (Vancouver-based)
Address: 1112 West Pender Street, Suite 500, Vancouver, BC V6E 2S1, Canada
Tel: 1-866-844-6783
http://www.toursbylocals.com/edgeofbeauty

Aegean Trails (Santorini Day Tours)
Address: Firá, 84100,Greece
Tel: +30 693 296 0062
http://santorini-privatetour.com/santorini-helicopter-tours

My Santorini (Pelican Travel Services)
Address: Firá, Santorini, 84700, Greece
Tel: +30 22860 22220
Fishing Tour:
http://www.mysantorini.com/Santorini-Fishing-Tour.html

Diving Tour:
http://www.mysantorini.com/Santorini-Diving-Tours.html

• 5 Days in Santorini! •

Enjoy this 5-day itinerary for a well-balanced and enjoyable experience! You can follow this itinerary to the letter, or you can modify and adjust for time, interest and/or preferences. Either way, have fun!

• Day 1 •

When you arrive in Santorini and get checked into your hotel accommodations (hopefully you arrive in the morning or early afternoon), have a short rest, get refreshed and renewed, then head out to see the **Museum of Prehistoric Thira** in Firá.

The museum has artifacts that are mostly from ancient Santorini as well as features from the island's various historical periods, dating from the 5th century to the Holy Roman Empire. It's a very interesting place to see, and a great way to kick off your time on the island.

Unless you're too jet-lagged or worn out from the day's traveling, after you see the museum, you can head north in Firá, where you'll find two wonderful villages: **Firostefani and Imerovigli**. Firostefani is a small Firá neighborhood, within walking distance of the city center. It's the **highest viewpoint** over the caldera and a great spot to check out this evening for the view of the lights at night. Imerovigli is a bit further north and features great luxury hotels, restaurants and other accommodations. We suggest asking a local for **tonight's dinner recommendation** in either of these great neighborhoods.

Afterward, head back to your hotel and get a good night's rest. Tomorrow awaits!

Museum of Prehistoric Thira
Address: Φηρά, Firá, 84700, Santorini, Greece
Tel: +30 2286 022217
http://www.santonet.gr/museums/prehistoric_museum.htm

• Day 2 •

After a quick breakfast at your hotel or at a nearby café, **head over to the picturesque town of Oia** (Greek: Οία). You can get there easily from the central bus station in Firá. Be sure to wear your good walking shoes, as getting around on foot is the way to go.

Once in Oia, go see the **Church of Panagia**, a gorgeous house of prayer; and the **Byzantine Castle Ruins,** which offers breathtaking views in addition to being an ancient ruin; and the **Naval Maritime Museum**, which occupies a restored and remodeled 19th century mansion. There are also loads of **specialty and gift shops**, **wineries** and **art galleries** around town that you may enjoy perusing.

You can lunch at **Mes Amis**, a charming **traditional European café** with great food, coffee and desserts.

It is important to keep in mind: Oia is a pretty expensive town for dining and accommodations, so as we mentioned earlier, if you're **on a budget**, you should consider staying elsewhere (see our **upcoming recommendations**) and perhaps bring picnic foods to Oia.

If you're not on a budget (or just feel like splurging), don't miss dinner tonight at **Ambrosia Restaurant** for some of the most delicious Mediterranean and Greek fare on the island.

Location Information:

Church of Panagia
Address: Main Square, Oia, Santorini, 84702, Greece

Mes Amis
Address: Oia, Santorini, Greece
Tel: +30 2286 027318
https://www.facebook.com/pages/Mes-Amis-Oia-Santorini/1438782759726337

Byzantine Castle Ruins
Address: Oia, Santorini, 84702

Naval Maritime Museum
Address: Oia, Santorini, 84702
Tel: +30 22860 71156
https://www.santorini.com/museums/naval_museum.htm

Ambrosia Restaurant
Address: Cliffside Terrace at Village Center, Oia, Santorini, 84702
Tel: +30 2286 071413
http://www.restaurant-ambrosia.com

• Day 3 •

If it isn't raining and the sun's shining brightly, let's **head to the beach today!**

Santorini has some of the most beautiful and unique **beaches** in all of Greece. Most are covered with black sand from the volcano. The popular beaches are: **Perivolos**, on the southern end of the island; **Kamari**, which is about six miles southeast of Firá and features attractive views of the shining rock at night; **Red Beach**, which is smaller and more crowded, but is arguably one of the most famous and beautiful beaches in Santorini; **Vlychada**, a long grey sand covered beach with sun lounges for relaxing; and **Perissa**, a black sand paradise about nine miles from Firá on Santorini's southeast side.

Plan to spend at least half a day at the beach, and don't forget the sunscreen!

And let's end this relaxing day with a visit to one of Santorini's many **wineries**. Try the **Santorini Wine Adventure Tour!**

Alternatively, you could also go **horseback riding**! Ride around the Santorini hills or along the marvelous beaches. It makes for a fun afternoon or evening activity, and you can even choose to ride on a donkey instead. Just check out **Aegean Wonder — Santorini Tours!**

Location Information:

Santorini Wine Adventure Tours
Address: Firá, 84700, Greece
Tel: +30 6932 960062 or +30 22860 34123
http://www.winetoursantorini.com

Aegean Wonder—Santorini Tours
Address: Fira, 84700, Greece
Tel: +30 698 059 3626
http://awsantorinitours.com/horseback-riding.html

• Day 4 •

The famed Greek Island of Crete is just a two-hour ride by ferry from Santorini and the day trip we're sending you on today! Crete is located in the southern part of the Aegean Sea and separates the Aegean from the Libyan Sea. **Heraklion** is the capital city and one of the largest in Greece itself.

The Palace of Knossos is the main tourist attraction in Crete. You should plan on spending at least half a day here. The palace once had over 1,200 rooms, some of which have been recreated to give you an idea of how stunning it was in its day. The first palace was built around 2000 BC, but was destroyed in an earthquake some 300 years later. An even larger palace was subsequently built but was again likely destroyed by the eruption of the volcano. It's an amazing and history-rich site.

Chania, Crete's second-largest city, is also popular with visitors. It has a truly picturesque Venetian harbor, the perfect spot for dinner and drinks, especially in the evening. There's also great shopping, interesting museums, and some of the nicest restaurants and hotels in Crete.

Have lunch at **Tavern Strata** while in Chania. We think reservations are ideal but not necessary, though there may be a wait. Pricing is fair, the atmosphere great and food delish!

You can also take a nice drive up a mountain road to see one of the most beautiful monasteries in Europe, the **Arkadi Monastery**. In 1866, hundreds of natives were killed here by Turkish troops occupying the island, and as such, it has become a symbol of their bid for independence.

In the evening, taking a walk along the **Samariá Gorge**, the longest gorge in Europe (about 10 miles), is definitely something you must do while in Crete. The views in the park are spectacular; well worth the effort to cover this great distance...well, at least you can try!

For dinner in Crete, our favorite spot is **Palmera Seaside Restaurant** in Crete's town of Hersonissos. Right on the sea with the most gorgeous views to take in as you dine on scrumptious homemade-style Mediterranean fare. Also a great spot for couples!

Location Information:

The Palace of Knossos
Address: Knossos Avenue, Heraklion, Crete, Greece
Tel: +30 2810 231940
http://www.heraklion.gr/en/ourplace/knossos/knossos.html

Tavern Strata
Address: Portou 54 | Old Venetian Harbor, Chania Town, Crete, 73100
Tel: +30 2821 093830
https://www.facebook.com/pages/Tavern-Strata/170295159714048

Arkadi Monastery
Address: Rethymnon, Rethymnon, Crete, 74100
Tel: +30 28310 83135
http://www.arkadimonastery.gr/index.php?homeen

Palmera Seaside Restaurant
Address: 25 Martiou, 14, Hersonissos, Crete, 70014
Tel: +30 2897 022481
http://www.palmeraseaside.gr

• Day 5 •

How about a visit to **Akrotiri** on your last day in Santorini? About 3,500 years old, this Minoan town is preserved in volcanic ash (similar to Italy's Pompeii), and located in the southern part of the island. The ruins are quite well preserved and you can check out cool frescoes and Minoan pottery work.

Go see the **Akrotiri Lighthouse** (Faros in Greek). The Greek Navy actively uses it so civilians can't go in, but it is a **great photo opp**.

Alternatively, you could go for that **helicopter ride** or take a **boat or hiking tour** today! See **Pelican Travel Services** and have some fun!

For lunch today, head over to **The Good Heart** for a fresh, homemade-style, delicious bite to eat.

And if the weather permits, you must visit **Open Air Cinema Kamari**, a great outdoor theater that plays great movies, serves food, snacks, and drinks. You can go in the evening and spend a relaxing time with good entertainment, food, and wine!

You can do dinner at the lovely **Asterias** before or after the movies. They serve traditional Mediterranean cuisine, one of our favorite restaurants by the sea in Santorini.

Location Information:

Akrotiri Lighthouse
Address: Lighthouse Road, Akrotiri, Greece

The Good Heart
Address: Faros Street, Akrotiri, 84700
Tel: +30 2286 082247

Open Air Cinema Kamari
Address: Santorini, 84700
http://www.cinekamari.gr

Asterias Restaurant
Address: Red Beach, Akrotiri, Greece
Tel: +30 2286 085234
http://asteriassantorini.com/?lang=en

My Santorini (Pelican Travel Services)
Address: Firá, Santorini, Firá, 84700
Tel: +30 22860 22220
http://www.mysantorini.com

• Best Places For Travelers on a Budget •

Bargain Santorini Sleeps

Oia's Sunset is the way to go if you are on a budget. Helpful, friendly management, breakfast and clean rooms — what more could you need?

Oia's Sunset
Address: Oia, Santorini, 84702, Greece
Tel: +30 22860 71420
http://www.oiasunset.com

One of the best budget-friendly spots in Firá, **Loizos** is in a peaceful cul-de-sac, just minutes from the city center and the edge of the caldera. Apartments range from standard to deluxe. Try to snag a room in the front, on the upper floor for a panoramic view of Kamari village, and the sea!

Loizos — Stylish Residences Santorini
Address: Firá, Thera, 84700, Greece
Tel: +30 2286 024046
http://www.loizos.gr

Centrally located near the Santorini airport, **Perissa Bay** offers indoor and outdoor pools, balconies and patios overlooking the mountains, the garden or pool. This budget-friendly hotel can arrange a variety of activities for you, like diving, jet skiing and other water sports. Great restaurants, cocktail bars and clubs are within walking distance.

Perissa Bay
Address: Perissa, 84703, Santorini
Tel: +30 2286 082191
http://www.perissabay.com

Bargain Santorini Eats

For really good eating on a budget, head over to **Chef's Garden** in Firá, a stylish spot open for breakfast, lunch and dinner with very friendly servers.

Chef's Garden
Address: Agiou Athanasiou, Fira, 84700, Santorini
Tel: +30 2286 022 277

Nikolas Taverna in Firá is a no-frills, inexpensive restaurant frequented by locals, with some of the most delicious food! It's one of our favorite spots on the island.

Nikolas Taverna
Address: Erythrou Stavrou, Firá, 15342, Santorini
Tel: +30 2286 024550

And meal prices are relatively reasonable at **Classico Cafe Restaurant** — great Italian/Mediterranean fusion fare with views that are to die for! And don't miss their delicious ice cream. They have a few locations on the island, but our favorite is on the Kamari boardwalk.

Classico Cafe Restaurant
Address: At the boulevard, Kamari, 84700, Santorini
Tel: +30 2286 023112
http://santorini-classico.gr/

• Best Places For Ultimate Luxury •

Luxury Santorini Sleeps

One of the most luxurious and stunning hotels on the island (and our top recommendation) is the **Canaves Oia Santorini**. Perched on one of the highest points of Santorini, the luxurious guest rooms and breathtaking views make this hotel a true dream!

Canaves Oia Santorini
Address: 84702, Oia, Santorini
Tel: +30 2286 071453
http://canaves.com

One of Santorini's best luxury hotels is **Katikies Hotel**. Consisting of a small collection of private rooms and suites, Katikies is perched on a cliffside with some of the most jaw dropping views in the world. They also happen to have some of the friendliest staff around.

Katikies Hotel Santorini
Address: Main Street, Oia, 84702, Santorini

Tel: +30 2286 071401
http://www.katikies.com

Another great place to stay in Oia is **Fanari Villas**. This well appointed hotel has a dozen villa-esque, cave-style suites and is an ideal locale for weddings, anniversary celebrations, etc. Members of the staff dress in all white, for a nice aesthetic touch.

Fanari Villas
Address: Oia 84702, Santorini
Tel: +30 2286 071008
http://fanarivillas.gr

Luxury Santorini Eats

Ambrosia Restaurant in Oia is our favorite restaurant for fine dining in Santorini. The views from the terrace (two to choose from) are stunning, and the food is scrumptious. This is a very popular spot so reservations are hard to get; book a table here well in advance of your trip.

Ambrosia Restaurant
Address: Cliffside Terrace at Village Center, Oia, Santorini, 84702
Tel: +30 2286 071413
http://www.restaurant-ambrosia.com

Santorini's Mystique Hotel houses the **Charisma Restaurant**, which offers dynamite Mediterranean cuisine. Definitely high end, Charisma is another hot spot, so you'll need to make your reservations well in advance.

Charisma Restaurant
Address: Thera, 84702, Santorini
Tel: +30 2286 071114
http://mystique.gr/charisma-restaurant

<u>Selene Restaurant</u> relocated from Firá to Pyrgos, Greek favorites are served here: lamb, rabbit, quail — all so delicious!

Selene Restaurant
Address: Pyrgos, 84700, Santorini
Tel: +30 22860 22249
http://www.selene.gr

• Santorini Nightlife •

Visitors to the island who are interested in Santorini's nightlife have a number of bars, live music, traditional Greek singing and dancing, as well as modern disco clubs to choose from!

Great Bars in Santorini

<u>Casablanca Soul</u> is a nice cocktail bar in Santorini, located on the rim of the caldera, it's the happening spot for nighttime fun on the island. Popular bands from around the world perform at Casablanca. The bar opens around 10:00 pm and closes when the last guests leave at dawn.

Casablanca Soul
Address: Ypapantis 12, Firá, Downtown, Thera, 84700, Santorini
Tel: +30 2286 027188
http://casablancasoul.com

Chilli Beach Bar is one of the most famous beach bars in Santorini. Located on the famous Perivolos Beach, it's one of the hottest destinations on the island and is sure to be loads of fun for you if you enjoy nightlife and like to party.

Chilli Beach Bar
Address: 84700, Thíra, Kikladhes, Santorini
Tel: +30 22860 82790

Another awesome bar in Santorini is the **Tango Bar.** On the way to the old port, it's one of the glitziest bars on the caldera, and great for having a party. A bit on the pricey side, it's a great spot to see and be seen!

Tango Bar
Address: Marinatou, Thera, 84700, Santorini
Tel: +30 697 449 8206
http://www.tangosantorini.gr

Great Clubs in Santorini

Enigma is a great, three-room club we like a lot. It's almost legendary on the island for modern disco and great drinks. Frequented by a range of age groups, everyone can have a good time at Enigma.

Enigma Club
Address: Thíra, Kikladhes, Santorini
Tel: +30 2286 022466
https://www.facebook.com/EnigmaClubSantorini

Koo Club is a definitive place to visit for a truly authentic Santorini experience!

Koo Club
Address: Firá, 84700, Thíra, Kikladhes, Santorini
Tel: +30 2286 022025
http://www.kooclub.gr

Great Live Music in Santorini

For the best live music and singing experience, don't miss the island's famous **"Souvlaki and Singing"** competition near the church in Oia. This event happens **every Sunday night** at 9:00 pm. They sing songs by famous Greek singers throughout the night (all genres) while guests partake of **endless amounts of souvlaki!** It's such a great time!

Church of Panagia
Address: Main Square, Oia, Santorini, 84702

Sky Lounge on Kamari Beach is another fabulous spot for great live music and a good time. It's a cozy restaurant/bar and live music venue with a modern décor. Good drinks and snacks are served.

Sky Lounge
Address: Kamari Beach, Kamari, 84700, Santorini
Tel: +30 6939 418960
http://www.santorini-skylounge.com

Another great option is **Dimitris Taverna**. Truly great on hot summer nights! They offer good eats and great entertainment from local dancers and musicians performing traditional Greek music.

Dimitris Taverna — Greek Nights
Address: Kamari, 84700, Santorini
Tel: +30 2286 032748
http://santorinidimitris.com

Great Theatre in Santorini

The White Door Theatro in Firá is a great interactive dinner theater where you're sure to have a great night! Traditional Greek fare like olives, cheese, salads and bread are included in the entrance charge.

The White Door Theatro
Address: Fira, 84700, Santorini
Tel: +30 2286 021770
http://www.whitedoorsantorini.com

• Conclusion •

Aside from the beautiful landscape and richly historic atmosphere, Santorini is a great place for a multitude of getaway activities: whether it's touring wineries, exploring ancient ruins, camping on the beach, hiking, scuba diving, window shopping or dining out, the island will not fall short of enchanting you!

We hope you've found our guide to the beautiful island of Santorini helpful and wish you a safe, happy and fun-filled trip to Greece!

Warm regards,

The Passport to European Travel Guides Team

Visit our Blog! Grab more of our signature guides for all your travel needs!

http://www.passporttoeuropeantravelguides.blogspot.com

★ **Join our mailing list** ★ to follow our Travel Guide Series. You'll be automatically entered for a chance to win a **$100 Visa Gift Card** in our monthly drawings! Be sure to respond to the confirmation e-mail to complete the subscription.

Passport to European Travel Guides is an eclectic team of international jet setters who know exactly what travelers and tourists want in a cut-to-the-chase, comprehensive travel guide that suits a wide range of budgets.

Our growing collection of distinguished European travel guides are guaranteed to give first-hand insight to each locale, complete with day-to-day, guided itineraries you won't want to miss!

We want our brand to be your official Passport to European Travel — one you can always count on!

Bon Voyage!

The Passport to European Travel Guides Team
http://www.passporttoeuropeantravelguides.blogspot.com

Made in the USA
San Bernardino, CA
07 February 2018